The Potter and the Clay

•

REFLECTIONS AND PRAYERS
FOR EVERYDAY LIVING

•

GLENNA OLDHAM
and paintings by
SYLVIA GRUBBS

Scripture quotations are from the New American Standard Bible,
The Lockman Foundation 1960, 1962, 1963, 1968, 1971, 1973, 1975, 1977.

©1986, Warner Press, Inc.

ISBN: 0-87162-446-X

All Scriptures are taken from the New American Standard
Bible unless otherwise noted.

Then I went down to the potter's house,
and there he was, making something on the wheel.
But the vessel that he was making of clay
was spoiled in the hand of the potter;
so he remade it into another vessel,
as it pleased the potter to make.
Then the word of the Lord came to me saying,
. . . Behold, like the clay in the potter's hand,
so are you in My hand.

JEREMIAH 18:3, 6

The Potter and the Clay

•

REFLECTIONS AND PRAYERS
FOR EVERYDAY LIVING

•

GLENNA OLDHAM
and paintings by
SYLVIA GRUBBS

To our children

Randy, Jana and Lora
Leta and Jonathan

A WORD TO THE READER

This book was born to say, in a simple way, that
there is an Answer for our problems, perplexities
and yearnings that spring from everyday life, and
that even the smallest prayer in the midst of our
living is a loving look at Christ.

Even though the answers herein from our Lord God
were spoken to a people of long ago in faraway
places, these same truths are ours today. The psalmist
wrote, "This will be written for the generations to
come, that a people yet to be created may praise the
Lord." So let us PRAISE THE LORD and write our names
before each of His Promises, claiming them for our own.

Come along, friend—let us walk the dusty roads and
seashores with the Master, listen from the mountainsides,
kneel at the foot of a cruel cross—and look into an
empty tomb. Let us sing with the children, HOSANNA
IN THE HIGHEST! Then let us lend ourselves well into
the hands of the Divine Potter.

Thank you for the pleasure of your company, dear reader,
and may your own needs be answered from Above,
friend talking to Friend.

GLENNA OLDHAM
and
SYLVIA GRUBBS

*H*eaven's harmony fills the air,
when the cry of the soul
becomes a prayer.

Relentlessly
You have pursued me, Lord,
though I did not hear your footfall
or feel the touch of your hand.
My ear did not catch the gentle sound
of Your voice—
but my heart did.

*W*hat do you think? If any
man has a hundred sheep,
and one of them has gone
astray, does he not leave the
ninety-nine on the mountains
and go and search for the one
that is straying? . . . And
when he has found it, he lays
it on his shoulders, rejoicing.

Matthew 18:12; Luke 15:5

How can it be, Dear Savior,
That you looked down through all of time
to this very moment—
and knew me
and loved me
and died for me.

Before I formed you in the womb I knew you. . . . The very hairs of your head are all numbered. . . . I am the good shepherd; and I know My own, and My own know Me . . . and I lay down My life for the sheep.
Jeremiah 1:5; Matthew 10:30;
John 10:14, 15

There was a young lad, I am told, who prayed,
"Our Father which art in heaven.
How'd you know my name?"
It's a great wonder for me, too, Lord!
Just to think—you not only know my name,
You know all about me—all my ways.
And still you love me.

I have redeemed you; I have
called you by name; you are
Mine! . . . I am the Lord your
God . . . your Savior. . . .
You are precious in my sight
. . . and I love you.

Isaiah 43:1, 3, 4

Teach me, Jesus,
and I shall throw my arms
around all you have said,
Claiming these promises, these truths, for my own.
And when doubts come pounding
at my heart's door, I shall fasten the latch
with the sure-strong Word of God.

I will instruct you and teach
you in the way which you
should go; I will counsel you
with My eye upon you. . . .
When you pass through the
waters, I will be with you. . . .
I am the Lord, your
Holy One.

Psalm 32:8; Isaiah 43:2, 15

We sing a beloved old hymn that says,
OH, TO BE LIKE THEE! BLESSED REDEEMER.
Is it true that we become like that which we love?
If only I could love you enough, Dearest Lord,
Enough to be so changed of heart—
TO BE LIKE THEE, BLESSED REDEEMER.
Amen.

t is enough for the disciple that he become as his teacher, and the slave as his master. . . . A new commandment I give to you, that you love one another, even as I have loved you.

Matthew 10:25; John 13:34

*It has been said that love is extravagant.
If so, then what is this impoverished meagerness
I have called love?
I have talked too much . . . too often, Lord.
Speak Your Love through my living,
everyday living—loving and caring
in a restless world that waits for You
unknowingly.*

*U*nless a grain of wheat falls
into the earth and dies, it
remains by itself alone; but if
it dies, it bears much fruit.

John 12:24

I love you, Lord.
And it is my dearest desire
that I may come to know you better.
That I may embrace
Your teachings,
Your way of love,
even the cross you died upon,
Until you are intricately woven
into the fabric of my life
like a thread of gold,
Joyously radiant.

*Y*ou do not know what you are asking for. Are you able to drink the cup that I drink. . . . For even the Son of Man did not come to be served, but to serve, and to give His life a ransom for many. . . . Come, follow me.

Mark 10:21, 38, 45

Lord,
there are days when I cannot feel You near me.
Then I remember—You are not a feeling.
You are my EVER-PRESENT
HEAVENLY FATHER.
ALLELUIA!

I AM WHO I AM. . . .
This is My name forever, and
this is My memorial-name to
all generations. . . . Is there
any God besides Me, or is
there any other Rock? . . . For
I, the Lord, do not change.
Exodus 3:14, 15; Isaiah 44:8;
Malachi 3:6

Turmoil is everywhere.
Uncertainty is camped all around.
Fear is a cold wind blowing in my face.
Dearest Lord, please give this wayfarer courage
to plant a mustard seed even now.

Do not fear, for I am with you; Do not anxiously look about you, for I am your God. I will strengthen you, surely I will help you. . . . . Do not tremble or be dismayed, for the Lord your God is with you wherever you go.

Isaiah 41:10; Joshua 1:9

*My searching soul has found so many questions
in life.
The voice of becoming cries from the depths
of my being for all the answers.
If I come to know the great truths of life,
and have knowledge of many things—
philosophies, laws, creeds, doctrines—
And I never come to know You,
Beloved Son of God,
then what have I gained?*

*For everyone who asks,
receives; and he who seeks,
finds; and to him who knocks,
it shall be opened. . . . I will
come in to him, and will dine
with him, and he with Me.*
Luke 11:10; Revelation 3:20

Lord Jesus,
Are you weary of finding this cup of mine dry?
It is so easy to become lost in my own plans
and problems.
So wrapped up in them—days run into weeks,
Weeks into months—and then it is my chosen
way of life.
Forgive me.
Dear Holy Spirit, fill my heart again.
Be Thou exalted over all I treasure—my dreams,
my likes and dislikes.
Be Thou glorified in my life.

I spoke to you, rising up early
and speaking, but you did not
hear, and I called you but you
did not answer. . . . And I
say to you, ask, and it shall be
given to you. . . . For I will
pour out water on the thirsty
land and streams on the
dry ground.
Jeremiah 7:13; Luke 11:9;
Isaiah 44:3

You are my wellspring, Lord!
And how greatly I am blessed
by tributaries of many loved ones
a source of effervescent joy!
Flow through my life, O Holy Spirit,
Ever-flowing, ever-cleansing
the backwaters of my mind.
ridding my soul of stagnation,
So that I, too, shall be a source
of your love.

He who believes in Me . . .
From his innermost being shall
flow rivers of living water.
John 7:38

My heart is the heart of a mountain-climber,
jubilant with expectancy,
savoring the wonders of each new summit.
I want to know more about God My Creator,
His creation and life.
O Jesus, come and walk with me
so that my searching soul may have
understanding
that brings love,
love that brings joy,
and joy that stays
through passing on every blessing.

The Helper, the Holy Spirit, whom the Father will send in My name, He will teach you all things. . . . Blessed are those who hear the word of God, and observe it.
John 14:26; Luke 11:28

*W*hat an awesome gift, Lord,
LOVE
a bouquet of wildflowers
clutched tightly in a tiny hand,
a note of remembrance from faraway,
a friendly call from down the street,
an encouraging hand on my shoulder,
. . . . a cross on a lonely hill.

By this all men will know that you are my disciples, if you have love for one another. . . . Greater love has no one than this, that one lay down his life for his friends. . . . For God so loved.

John 13:35; 15:13; 3:16

Hosanna in the Highest!
How good You are to me.
How blessed am I!
Day upon day Your loving mercies
and exceeding kindnesses surround me.
Now let me run
and do something good, something
wonderful
for my Lord and my God.

*Be still and know that I am
God. . . . . learn from Me, for
I am gentle and humble
in heart.*
Psalm 46:10 (KJV); Matthew
11:29

My Dear-Worthy Lord,
it is my desire to lay at Your feet
a beautiful offering—an acceptable gift—
for the King of Kings and Lord of Lords!
Though it may cost me comfort, honor,
health, or wealth.
Rise, O Lord,
Into Your proper place of excellency in my life.

Your loyalty is like a morning
cloud, and like the dew which
goes away early. . . . I delight
in loyalty rather than
sacrifice, and in the
knowledge of God rather than
burnt offerings. . . . But go
and learn what this means, I
desire compassion, and
not sacrifice.

Hosea 6:4, 6; Matthew 9:13

Today I heard in a bird's song,
"Top of the morning to you there."
And in the whispers of an evening breeze,
"It's good to be with you, my child."
It was not a burning bush, Lord,
Nevertheless, I removed my shoes.

He who is of God hears the
words of God. . . . *He who*
has ears to hear, let him
hear. . . . To you it has been
granted to know the mysteries
of the kingdom of heaven.
John 8:47; Matthew 11:15; 13:11

Whisper to my heart again and again, Lord,
that life is now, today.
I pray that all my smiles may not be borrowed
from yesterday—or even tomorrow,
Always hungering for something from long ago,
faraway—or yet about to be.
Give me a deep awareness of each moment's
holiness,
and the knowledge of Your presence.

What you have, hold fast until I come. . . . And he who overcomes, and he who keeps My deeds until the end . . . I will give him the morning star.

Revelation 2:25, 26, 28

O God,
I pray that I would be known as one who
lives lovingly.
Let me ease more deeply into the
sheer comfort of Your presence each day,
until I feel at home.
And when I die, Lord, may I have
a twinkle in my eye!

*Truly I say to you, whoever
does not receive the kingdom
of God like a child shall not
enter it at all.*

Mark 10:15

Good Master,
teach me to listen with my heart,
for the heart knows and understands much
that reason can never know.
There are so many words unspoken,
So many songs unsung.
Let my hearing be tuned to the sounds
and songs of the lost . . . the lonely.

And whoever . . . gives to one
of these little ones even a cup
of cold water to drink, truly I
say to you he shall not lose his
reward. . . . Whoever loses his
life for My sake, he is the one
who will save it.

Matthew 10:42; Luke 9:24

Dear Friend Jesus, yesterday we walked together,
and my soul was lifted high.
I saw as my blinded eyes had never seen
the awesome beauty and wonder
of Your sovereign power, truth, and glory!
Where are You today, Lord?
Why are You silent
in this deep valley of loneliness and loss?
Surely You hear the sounds
of my brokenheartedness.

You are My servant, I have chosen you and not rejected you. . . . I will not forget you. Behold, I have inscribed you on the palms of My hands.

Isaiah 41:9; 49:15, 16

Almighty God of my Life and All Creation,
I stand here under the stars
drenched with a great quietness.
I come to this serene and spacious place
to find a fresh spirit—a cleansing
of my soul.
The world is like a maze with many paths
that lead nowhere; just let me stay here
until I find myself in You.
Then lead me home.

I will give you a new heart. . . .
and I will put My Spirit within
you and cause you to walk in
My statutes. . . . I am the way,
and the truth, and the life.
Ezekiel 36:26, 27; John 14:6

*I f I follow
closely,
will You not make known to
me
Your ways, my Lord?
Then I will see my own failure to love
and nothing else . . .*

I am the light of the world; he
who follows Me shall not walk
in the darkness, but shall have
the light of life.

John 8:12

Jesus my Lord wept.
And, Dear God, forbid that I should not.
In the distance I can see a wayward one
looking longingly toward home.
Even from afar I see the hurt, regret,
and sorrow.
Old wounds in my own heart begin to ache,
even so—
Good Master, help me run and meet him.

Freely you received,
freely give.
Matthew 10:8

*Forgive me, Lord, if ever I should wrap myself
in pharisaic robes when I see another fall.
In no way am I greater
because of another's weakness.
At the most it only turns the eyes
of the crowd away from my own fraility.
Few of us would ever think of hurting someone
physically
But too many times have we used the power
of "talk" to kill.
Here, Lord, take these stones I hold.*

He who is without sin among you, let him be the first to throw a stone. . . . For in the way you judge, you will be judged; and by your standard of measure, it shall be measured to you.

John 8:7; Matthew 7:2

*M*y Sovereign God,
Lord of my life,
Thank You for Your Holy Word
sent from days long past.
It is as if even then
You saw me today
and knew my need.

It is written, "Man shall not live on bread alone, but by every word that proceeds out of the mouth of God.". . . Therefore every one who hears these words of Mine, and acts upon them, may be compared to a wise man, who built his house upon the rock. . . . Heaven and earth will pass away, but My words will not pass away.

Matthew 4:4; 7:24; Mark 13:31

As I stand before the mirror
of Your Holy Word, Lord,
May Heaven's Light fall upon any pretense,
sham, or such that lingers in the shadows
of my life. Make me genuine—
Real through and through.
I would be a vessel that has lent itself well
to the hands of the Divine Potter.

And I will ask the Father, and He will give you another Helper, that He may be with you forever; that is the Spirit of truth.

John 14:16, 17

I am distressed with my lack of enthusiasm,
joy
and vision.
When did I lose them?
Surely some thief has stolen them away.
I fear that my serving will be to no avail
without these treasures of my soul.
Restore that which I have lost, Dear Master.

The sower went to sow his seed . . . some fell beside the road. . . . and other seed fell among the thorns; and the thorns grew up with it, and choked it out. . . . These are the ones who have heard, and as they go on their way they are choked with worries and riches and pleasures of this life. . . . Return to Me, and I will return to you. . . . Bring the whole tithe into the storehouse . . . I will . . . open for you the windows of heaven, and pour out for you a blessing until there is no more need.

Luke 8:5, 7, 14; Malachi 3:7, 10

Here I am again, Lord . . .
bringing this burden to you.
It is a heavy load that bends me low.
How many times have I laid it down
at your feet?
Yet, over and over,
inevitably,
I find myself hindered by this
same persistent burden.

Come to Me, all you who are weary and are heavy laden, and I will give you rest. . . . For my yoke is easy and My load is light.

Matthew 11:28, 30

Lord, Lord—
Why?

Will the clay say to the potter, "What are you doing?". . . It is I who made the earth, and created man upon it. I stretched out the heavens with My hands. . . ." Come near to Me, listen to this: From the first I have not spoken in secret. . . . I am the Lord your God . . . . who leads you in the way you should go. . . . .

Behold, I have refined you.

Isaiah 45:9, 12; 48:10, 16, 17

*The secret of many a person's strength is
in having a friend—
One who will come when all the world
has left.
Such a fortunate one am I, Lord.
With marvelous grace You sent Your Love,
strong arms and loving hearts
carried my pallet
and laid me gently at Your feet.*

*A*nd when he saw him, he felt compassion, and came to him . . . and took care of him. . . . Go and do the same. . . . You shall love the Lord your God with all your heart, and with all your soul, and with all your strength, and with all your mind; and your neighbor as yourself.

Luke 10:27, 33, 34, 37

Like the blind man at Jericho,
I, too, sat by the road of life crying,
          Jesus,
      Have mercy on me!
I only remember reaching out
          for Him.

Who is the one who touched
Me? . . . Someone did touch
Me. . . . Daughter, your faith
has made you well; go in
peace. . . . Go home to your
people and report to them what
great things the Lord has done
for you, and how He had mercy
on you.

Luke 8:45, 46, 48; Mark 5:19

Thank you, Lord,
for many blessings
and for the quiet joy of this twilight hour.
In it I find a special blessedness,
peace
drifting down
settling
Oh, so silently upon my soul.
With all this glory here
and heaven waiting there
My heart is made to wonder why we who were
made to love should fluster and fuss
over such trivial matters of life.

*L*et not your heart be troubled;
believe in God, believe also in
Me. . . . For I go to prepare a
place for you . . . that where I
am, there you may be
also. . . . Peace I leave with
you; My peace I give to you.

John 14:1, 2, 3, 27

I am so glad to be on my way heavenward.
But I am most happy to be alive TODAY, Lord,
here in this place, now at this moment,
Alive in CHRIST!
For the happiest people I know are those
who are alive to LIFE—
Breathing in the fragrance of flowers,
Hearing the rhythm of rain
and even the silence of falling snow,
Feeling the touch of a tender hand
and even the touch of a soul.

These things I have spoken to you, that My joy may be in you, and that your joy may be made full.

John 15:11

Lord,
Enclose me in the cocoon of your Holy Spirit.
Wrap and hide me that I shall be seen no more.
Then, even as the dusty little caterpillar
gives himself up for death, yet comes
bursting into life again,
New, beautiful, and free,
So shall I!
Alleluia!

If you abide in My word, then you are truly disciples of Mine; and you shall know the truth, and the truth shall make you free. . . . You shall be free indeed. I am Alpha and Omega, the beginning and ending . . . I am He that liveth, and was dead; and behold, I am alive forevermore, Amen.

John 8:31, 32, 36;
Revelation 1:8, 18 (KJV)

*Worthy art Thou, our Lord
and our God, to receive glory
and honor and power; for
Thou didst create all things,
and because of Thy will they
existed, and were created.*

Revelation 4:11